CALL ME FOOL

CALL ME FOOL

poems

WILLIAM TROWBRIDGE

Red Hen Press | Pasadena, CA

Book design by Mark E. Cull

Library of Congress Cataloging-in-Publication Data

Names: Trowbridge, William, 1941– author.
Title: Call me fool / William Trowbridge.
Description: First edition. | Pasadena, CA : Red Hen Press, [2022]
Identifiers: LCCN 2022006667 | ISBN 9781636280462 (paperback) | ISBN
 9781636280813 (ebook)
Subjects: LCGFT: Poetry.
Classification: LCC PS3570.R66 C35 2022 | DDC 811/.54—dc23/eng/20220224
LC record available at https://lccn.loc.gov/2022006667

The National Endowment for the Arts, the Los Angeles County Arts Commission, the Ahman-
son Foundation, the Dwight Stuart Youth Fund, the Max Factor Family Foundation, the Pasade-
na Tournament of Roses Foundation, the Pasadena Arts & Culture Commission and the City of
Pasadena Cultural Affairs Division, the City of Los Angeles Department of Cultural Affairs, the
Audrey & Sydney Irmas Charitable Foundation, the Kinder Morgan Foundation, the Meta &
George Rosenberg Foundation, the Albert and Elaine Borchard Foundation, the Adams Family
Foundation, the Riordan Foundation, Amazon Literary Partnership, the Sam Francis Founda-
tion, and the Mara W. Breech Foundation partially support Red Hen Press.

First Edition
Published by Red Hen Press
www.redhen.org

ACKNOWLEDGMENTS

Thanks are due to the following periodicals in whose pages these poems first appeared:

American Journal of Poetry: "Call Him Mr. Lucky," "Fool Under the Big Top," "Mutiny on the Bounty: The Secret Report"; *Green Mountains Review*: "Fool at High Noon"; *I-70 Review*: "Fool in the Light Brigade," "Fool Falls Ill," "Fool Joins the Children's Crusade, Spring 1212," "Fool of the 7th Cavalry," "Fool Takes Charge," "Fool Undertakes a Holy Mission," "Fool Visits the All-New Heaven," "Tattered Fool"; *Rattle*: "Fool Invents the Piano, 1250 A.D.," "Robin Fool and His Disconsolate Men"; and *Sugar House Review*: "Immortal Fool."

For Bob Walkenhorst,
musician, painter, writer,
and amigo

Contents

The fool is not a mere safety valve for the suppressed instincts of the bully: he provides a subtler balm for the fears and wounds of those afflicted with their inferiority complex, the greater part of humanity if we may believe our psychologists. It is all very well to laugh at the buffeted simpleton: we too are subject to the blows of fate, and of people stronger and wiser than ourselves, in fact we *are* the silly Clown, the helpless Fool. How comforting then to be persuaded that the blows are always harmless, that the victim is never hurt, above all that Death himself is a hoax and that the whole world does not bear the tree on which Markolf can be hanged.

—Enid Welsford,
The Fool: His Social and Literary History

Proem: Immortal Fool

Death has to admit it's impossible
to kill Fool—not unless the killer

rubs out all humanity, a task that makes
even him too tired to think about.

It's playing whack-a-mole: kill him
in Athens, and he surfaces in Dresden.

Bump him off there, and he's sighted
in East Chicago, South Philly, and all

points west. Even if Death could
get him to kill himself, he'd pop up

again, tripping over his feet,
stumbling off the nearest curb,

dropping another wrench into
decorum's fragile gearbox. Too bad

there's not some secret weapon,
thinks Death: a Fool-piercing .44

magnum, double load. "Blam,"
says Death, air-firing from the hip.

"Blam! You're dead, Fool," he tells
his shadow, holstering a bony finger.

CALL ME FOOL

Call Him Mr. Lucky

Fool recalls his demotion from archangel
to something they called an archetype after he
was flimflammed by Lucifer and his buddies,

who seemed to have a viable way out of
a place where everyone's locked in orbit
around The Almighty, who likes his hallelujahs

chorused non-stop, like on a cracked LP.
But making Hell a heaven didn't fly,
and now he's on earth, buying Florida

swampland, phony Rolexes, and weekend
ski trips to Uganda. His franchise restaurant,
which offers only plain or raisin toast,

has yet to catch on, and his stock picks
followed Enron down the drain. He tells
himself his luck's bound to change,

says so even when he cuts off both hands
on his workshop band saw and can't
turn the door knob to go for help, finally

throwing himself out a plate-glass window,
which costs him his right ear. "But then I met
a man who had no arms," he recites to himself,

which he read in a prayer book a salesman
swore once belonged to the Apostle Paul.
God really does work in mysterious ways,

especially for archetypes, he thinks, trying
to hold his breakfast coffee with the hooks
another salesman said work just like hands.

Fool Helps Create the Earth

God decides to create something nice
in the void to make up for having to

concoct Hell and pitch the rebel angels
into it. "How about a jazzy new throne?"

he asks Fool, who shrugs and sighs,
suggesting something more bountiful.

"Well," says God, "maybe a mighty
fortress, like in that hymn." When Fool

notes that it hasn't been written yet,
God admits His omniscience keeps Him

jumping the gun but says a big fortress
would still be nice. "What about

a beautiful garden," says Fool, "with
cockatoos and flamingos, pomegranates

and palm fronds—and a beautiful couple
to enjoy it all." God thinks that sounds

pretty boring. "How 'bout putting apples
in there," He says, "and if they eat just

one—which my omniscience tells me
they will—I get to kick some more ass,

might even invent some new stuff:
sin, death, maybe even madness.

When Fool suggests that doesn't sound
very nice, he finds himself the lone

human on earth, memory scrubbed,
plunked under a tree of ripe Ambrosias.

Pleistocene Fool

When Fool's friends noticed some chips
and scratches he'd made on the cave wall
with stray spear chucks, it dawned on them

that they'd never seen anything quite
so graceful-looking, so evocative. He was
honored with a new word: "eep" (artist).

Members from other caves came to admire
his masterpiece. Some saw a deer in it,
some a mammoth, some a buxom woman.

Wherever they moved, the eyes seemed
to follow them, a feature they agreed
distinguished "eep" from aper, and why

they clubbed to death some local wannabes.
Fool, now revered clan-wide and getting paid
large sums of hind quarters and axe heads

for even talking about his work, grew
aloof and oversensitive, demanding
larger fees and greater adulation. Though

a few insisted all they saw were random
chips and scratches any fool could make,
Fool's demands grew more excessive.

The elders might have killed him but for awe
of the magic powers he claimed his art
endowed him with, immortality for one.

Given that, they asked him to quell
the latest menace, a raging cave bear,
with this mighty art they called "Deap."

He was to "Deap" the bear, a word that could also mean, "meat," "nudge" "hello" "nostril"—and a little later, "dead eep."

David and Goliath: The Real Story

Annoyed at being struck so rudely
with a rock, Goliath stomps David flat
as liver paté. Saul orders up posters
for a new hero candidate to save

the Israelites. Fool, fired from his job
as apprentice shepherd after losing
the herd to Phoenician con men, applies
and, due to a lack of other applicants,

gets the job. He's issued a sling-shot,
canvas shield, and a crash course
in combat moves by a retired mime.
At first, Goliath hardly notices

the little man in the clownish outfit,
who delivers his war-boast in a whisper.
When Goliath bends down to ask him
to repeat, Fool shrieks, "Leave this land,

or I won't be responsible!" Goliath, amused,
plays along, dropping to his knees to beg
for mercy. Fool's moved to pity, recalling
all the times he's had to take such bows.

"There, there," he says, patting a huge
hand. Goliath can't hold back a tear.
"You want *me* for a friend?" he utters.
Fool, who's never heard those words

addressed to him, nods, and soon
the two go forth to preach friendship
to the antagonists, who, after listening
politely and consulting their elders,

stone them to pulp before concocting
their respective tales of heroic David
and martyred Goliath, then muster
arms for the next day's glorious fray.

Fool Undertakes a Holy Mission

Because Moses is busy chasing down
rumors of a golden calf, he orders Fool
up Mount Sinai to find the burning bush
and report, straight from the horse's mouth,

what God's latest tantrum's all about.
Arriving topside, Fool finds nothing
but a field of shrubs. Baffled, he lights
one on fire in hopes it will attract God

like chicken innards do those big catfish.
After the fire goes out uneventfully,
Fool tries searching the ground for clues.
All he finds is a pile of whitened fox feces,

which, when he inspects it closely, resembles
a grandpa sporting a snow-white beard,
a lot like God's. Fool, cradling his find
back down the mountain, discovers Moses

glumly watching a golden-calf orgy. "So you
thought they'd fall down and worship this pile
of shit in place of getting smashed, dancing,
and fucking their brains out?" Moses demands.

Fool explains that the shit part's irrelevant,
that the pile's an icon, revealing God's
purity and goodness. "Take a closer look,"
he says. Disgusted, Moses cobbles up a set

of rules he hopes will end the debauchery,
chisels them on a couple of flat stones,
and declares God sent them. Drowned out,
migraine throbbing, he retires to take a nap.

Fool Delivers the Sermon on the Mount

Thanks to a learner on the Holy Switchboard,
Fool got assigned to preach the big sermon.

He couldn't figure out how everyone
would hear him, he was so high up

and the crowd so vast, but he hoped
those in front could relay his message.

He tried to loosen things up with a joke about
three Pharisees in a bar, but nobody seemed

to get it. Consulting the Holy Bullet Points,
he began by letting the meek know they'd

inherit the earth, once they got the nod
form the Philistines, Hittites, and Egyptians.

He skipped the no-pearls-before-swine
mandate, since he'd found swine always

opt for the swill. Turning the other cheek
puzzled him. Wouldn't it work better

to flash both cheeks at once? He agreed
that the Gate was narrow and they suffer

an unholy host of enemies to try
loving, which usually turns them nastier.

After half the crowd had walked off,
some offering unchristian gestures,

he decided to close on a positive note:
"So, anybody up for loaves and carp?"

Fool Incarnate

Several years after the Crucifixion,
Fool's walking dully along, when
somebody notes his amazing likeness

to Jesus. Soon, word spreads that
the Second Coming's come early.
When Fool tries to explain he hasn't

died, everyone rejoices that the prophesy's
come true, that now the Roman yoke
will crumble with the Empire, that milk

and honey, decent wine, too, will be
franchised nationwide. People crowd in,
beseeching Fool to heal a few lepers,

raise dead Uncle Amos, strut across
the Sea of Galilee. The disciples
hesitate, then join the celebration.

"How will we deal with the oppressor
and his stooges now that *we're*
holding the big stick," everyone asks.

"Be nice?" offers Fool, taken aback
from actually being noticed. The cheers
die down. "No beheading? No stoning?

No rack and/or screw?" they ask.
"No death to their children and their
children's children?" When Fool

brings up that tiresome rumor about
a Golden Rule, they suspect Christ's
still a sob sister, that he might even

have turned Sodomite. "Maybe we
could give them a good talking to,"
Fool says, as the first nail goes in.

Fool the Hun

Training for Hunship, Fool was afraid
to get on a horse, much less a steed,
much less ride full-speed while shooting

arrows from it with uncanny accuracy.
When his instructor shouted, "Show me
your Hun face!" Fool could only look

like he was about to throw up. And he
wasn't thrilled about raping, pillaging,
and burning, though he liked campfires,

which made him mix up the prescribed order:
"Idiot!" snarled his instructor. "Burn *after*
you rape and pillage." "Hey, newt brain,"

someone said, "if you can't throw a spear,
try catching this one," which, shockingly,
Fool did, one after another— the same

with clubs, axes, arrows, fire balls,
even stones launched from a catapult.
"Moron!" barked the instructor. "You

got it backwards again: Huns throw,
the others catch—in their heads, guts,
and fleeing asses. If everybody caught

like you, what would life be like? No
cries of terror, no trampled infants,
no rape, pillage, and burn—only peace

and plenty, followed by more peace and
more plenty. We'd die of boredom." Fool
thought, then, throwing a pole ax, said,

"Sorry. Don't catch this." "You've got it, finally," his instructor gasped, smiling his last smile. "Huns will rule the world!"

The Alchemist's Apprentice

It takes a golden heart, Fool's told,
free from the merest fleck of sin,
from the slightest tilt toward mischief
no worse than, say, kicking a beggar,
to turn base metal into something worth
any number of living things, including
your brother, your wife and children,
and children those children might have
and children *they* might have
or think about having, consciously
or unconsciously, and their dogs,
cats, goats, fish, monkeys, sheep,
and any other pets and livestock,
including those little yellow budgies
that go "ka-roo, ka-roo" when you talk
baby talk to them; and babies, too,
in case you thought they weren't included
in "children"; and fetuses down to
those who are just one cell, that could
still grow into frogs or camelopards,
which, along with cells, are also listed.

"How's rat catching pay?" asks Fool,
lead heart thumping in its cauldron.

The Pied Fool of Hamelin

Walking alone through the woods one day,
Fool finds a flute among the dead leaves.
When he picks it up and puts it to his lips,
a beguiling melody comes out, though

he's never played a note before. When he
arrives in Hamelin, he plays the flute
in hopes of earning money for a meal
and place to sleep. But with the music,

rats appear, hundreds of them, black,
greedy-eyed, their noses bristly and avid.
The townspeople fear Fool might be
a Jew, come from some Jew place to spread

plague and famine, that he could make
them dance in the square till they thrash
themselves to death, then pipe the children
off to mix their blood in matzo balls

for Jewry's heathen feasts. He senses
something might be wrong, that the baleful
stares, the raised pitchforks and sickles
signal it could be time to busk elsewhere.

Fool Joins the Children's Crusade, Spring 1212

It made good sense to him, much like Lucifer's
plan to make hell a heaven: defeat the Muslim
kingdoms by following Nicholas of Cologne

& Co. from Germany over the Alps to Genoa,
where God would dry up the sea before them.
Then they'd stroll on to the Holy Land, gentling

Muslims into Christians, bringing peace
through love. Nicholas received his charge
from an angel, who explained that, so far,

Crusaders failed because their hearts
were sinful. So, logically, children should
take their place. When two-thirds of the 7,000

died like winter flies and God, it seemed,
forgot or changed his mind about the sea,
Fool's faith stayed firm—even when

Pope Innocent III told the rest to go home
and Nicholas, who kept on, died and Fool
and Nicholas' father were tried and hanged

on behalf of outraged parents of the fallen.
On the fatal drop, it dawned on Fool that
boats might have been the wiser choice.

Fool Invents the Piano, 1250 A.D.

Like the monkey that accidentally typed *Hamlet*,
Fool, tinkering in his workshop, constructed
an exact likeness of a Steinway concert grand,

which he called the "Making-Sounds-with-Little-
Hammers-on-Wires-Machine." It looked impressive,
but he was puzzled about what to do with it.

It was too big and complicated to be a doorstop
and too heavy and lopsided to be a wheelbarrow,
especially with those little brass wheels, so he

tried using it to scare rats out of the hayloft.
But the rats weren't impressed, and he sprained
his back winching it up. Fool pushed on

the levers to make high sounds and low ones,
wondering why he'd made some levers black.
Neighbors, hearing eerie noises from his house,

suspected Fool of conjuring evil spirits
to cast spells on them. Several broke out
in goat-shaped rashes, others began speaking

gibberish. Soon, Fool found himself trussed atop
his machine, which was then dumped into a lake,
as Bartok's Piano Concerto No. 1 dawned on him.

Fool in Plague Time
—Siena, 1347

For protection, Fool joins the Flagellants,
who claim their penance encourages God
to spare them from earthly harm. The more
lashes, the purer the soul, the safer the body.
This *really hurts*, he thinks, after a few swats.

When he sees some of his fellow Flagellants
falling dead in the streets, he decides to try
just praying. But all he gets is a busy signal,
followed by a nasal voice saying the line
is no longer in service. As a last resort, Fool

tries washing instead of flagellation:
the cleaner the body, the safer the body?
He scrubs down twice a day and remains
healthy, as the plague continues to rage.
A few people decide to join him, soon

forming what they christen "the Scrubbedites,"
all of whom remain odor and plague free.
But the unwashed residents, including
the plaguey Flagellants, declare bathing
a Satanic ritual. The church decides

to star Fool and his Scrubbedite cohorts—
plus assorted Jews, gays, and other pariahs
in an *auto-da-fe*, hoping to please Him enough
to earn deliverance. Aflame, they remind
the archbishop of candles on a holy day.

Captain Fool Sails to the New World

Rejected to sail the *Pinta*, *Nina*
or *Santa Maria*, Fool, known by
his Spanish name, El Bufon, gets
assigned to captain *La Disgracia*,
a leaky, decommissioned frigate,
to help Columbus make history.

Thrown off course by foul weather
and faulty navigation, Fool makes
port at a small Caribbean island
whose inhabitants, good-natured
and weaponless, offer seafood,
breadfruit, and carefree sex.

Soon Fool and his crew commit
the unpardonable sin of colonizers:
going native. *Spain schmain*,
they think as they cavort among
the palms, sea breezes, laughter,
and plentitude of welcoming thighs—

till the *Nina* arrives. Its captain orders
the island cleansed by the standard
means of rape, pillage, murder,
enslavement, and Christianity. Chained
to the mainmast, Fool threatens
to report these abuses to the king.

Robin Fool and His Disconsolate Men

The snag arose right away: the rich
had troops and portcullises, making it
very risky to rob them. And the poor
were supposed to *receive* the swag, not

surrender it. So Fool decided they'd
rob the not-so-rich. However, rob them
enough and they become poor. Give
enough to the poor and, after a while,

they become the rich—a dispiriting treadmill.
Alan-a-Dale, the men's minstrel, tried to
make up a song about it but couldn't think
of a good lyric. Little John grew morose,

and Friar Tuck doubled his windy prayers.
Fool suggested they get into forest crafts:
whittled whistles and bowls, leaf pillows,
boar-tusk pipe bowls, rabbits' feet.

"Bowls and pillows, bowls and pillows,"
sang Alan-a-Dale, then faltered. Fool
suggested they could use a catchy slogan.
"Shop here or we kill you," offered Little John.

They considered, "Don't settle for that
crappy town stuff when you can buy
from the Merry Men." Too long, muttered
Will Scarlet. "And not all of us are men,"

chimed in Maid Marian. "How about,
'You wanna buy this?'" Fool suggested.
Though no one saluted when they ran it
up the flagpole, the progeny of King John

and his pal the Sheriff of Nottingham
later weaponized the concept, deploying
the first ad agency, which allowed them
to rob pretty much everybody.

King of Fools

Through a series of gaffs and bloody intrigues,
Fool, clueless as veal on the hoof, finds himself
spring-boarded from assistant rat catcher

to king in a small eighteenth-century European country
whose present government has generously paid
to have its name withheld from this poem.

Because Fool's shy about giving orders,
the vipers and toadies who constitute his court
infer the Royal will from his speech inflections

and body language, which are invariably translated
into the courtiers' ambitions, while Fool works
on pronouncing his h's and remembering names.

After dozens of public quarterings and an enforced
famine, a ghoul appears in slapped-up engravings.
It's carving up an infant at its banqueting table

by a row of disemboweled victims impaled on poles.
The top four of its buck incisors read "F-O-O-L."
"Down with Fool!" hears Fool, who abdicates

politely as a dinner guest who's sat in the wrong chair.
"Bang," go the seven barrels of the firing squad
not long after Fool asks what the blindfold's for.

Fool in the Light Brigade

When Fool heard it would be
a surprise attack, a charge into
the Russians' strength, cannons
on three sides and riflemen

surrounding, he wondered—
considering canister shot,
grape shot, and mini-ball ripping
through the air by the metric ton,

some of which could well pass
through him and his charger Reggie—
if the tactic might be imprudent.
But he'd heard the gripping speech

by Lord Cardigan, who would
lead the charge. Fool pictured
his tombstone, inscribed for a hero:
Cpl. Fool—Sic Nates Mundi,

or so he recalled from Latin class.
At the command—sabres raised
and lances lowered, cannons
to the right of them, cannons

to the left of them, cannons in front—
into the valley of death rode
the 599, since Fool, though witless,
wasn't crazy.

Mutiny on the *Bounty*: The Secret Report

Captain Fool was charged to search
the Pacific for breadfruit, which would
provide cheap food for the Empire.

When a typhoon struck, he ordered
everyone to safety below. His kindness
prevented the need for canings, floggings,

and keel haulings. Instead: days off,
best-swabbing awards, song fests,
shuffleboard, and extra grog. When they

reached Tahiti and the crew went native,
Fool joined the luau, wooed a wahini. But
his men had grown suspicious, still

conditioned to life in the Royal Navy—
its foot-on-the-neck discipline, its hardtack,
punk water, and furry meat. Fool

could be an enemy agent, who'd "kindly"
steer them into some Spanish port,
where they'd be killed or Catholicized.

Mutiny ensued, with Captain Fool
and a few loyals cast off in a lifeboat
as the *Bounty* set sail for England,

its crew expecting grateful adulation.
When they arrived, the Admiralty tried
all for mutiny and theft, sentencing them

to be hanged. Meanwhile, Fool arrived,
having piloted his grateful crew across
three thousand miles of open sea.

The Crown hailed him as hero of the Empire,
till his "gross and flagrant leniency" was uncovered
and he had to join the others on the yardarm.

In 1823, after Inventing a Flush Toilet,
Fool Discovers Penicillin, X-Rays, Plastic, and Super Glue

In his lab, Fool leaves some cultivated staphylococci
in a bowl before taking off on a two-week vacation.

When he returns, he finds a fluffy white mass
has stifled its growth. As the mass grows, it turns

dark green, then black, then bright yellow. Queasy,
and hoping to save his staphylococci, Fool tosses it

into his newly invented toilet, which, despite
numerous adjustments, still backfires geysers.

So he turns to fiddling with tubes and gasses,
and discovers a new ray, one that lets him see

his foot bones underneath the skin. Fool thinks
it would be an ideal aid to fitting shoes

or perhaps make a racy pair of novelty glasses,
neither concept impressing potential investors.

Undaunted, Fool mixes assorted chemicals
in his basement and comes up with something

clear as glass but pliable and lighter, which he
refines into a highly sticky substance he believes

would hold hair-pieces in place longer. He decides
the compound could be put into small tubes

and sold in beauty salons and barber shops.
After its reception, he flees town and settles

in a new state, where he hopes to continue work
on his toilet and what he calls a "Veg-O-Matic."

Fool Takes Charge

Due to a clerical error, Fool was appointed
a colonel in the Army of the Potomac.
Known to his men as Old Shit-for-Brains,
Fool, ordered by General Grant to flank
the enemy, heard "thank." Puzzled about
what to thank them for, he sent a messenger
to thank them for being good and true
soldiers. The rebels, not wanting to be
out-maneuvered, answered in kind. Fool
met their compliment with more thanks,
and soon both sides were sharing smokes,
songs, and pictures of wives and children,
a few even mugging in exchanged caps—

till word got back to the higher-ups, who
ordered an immediate halt to levity
and a return to battle the way sane men
do it. Fool, proud of his thanking attack
and thrilled about his many new friends,
spent the rest of the war in the stockade,
scrubbing out latrines and grease pits.

Call Me Fool

Fool believes he was signing up to help
load the *Pequod*, when he notices the skyline

receding. "Avast," barks a whiskered man
called Stubb. "Hye ye up to the fore-royal yard

and lend a hand with the royal." When Fool
looks baffled, he's thought to be too stupid

to unfurl sails. He's reassigned to stand
watch at the masthead and "sing out"

when he spots a whale, especially the one
that makes the captain so scary. Perched

on two narrow boards 100 feet above deck,
Fool's eager to spot anything that will

get him back down. "It's Moby Dick!"
he shouts at a whitecap. After that,

he's assigned to swab the poop deck,
which he's relieved to find is presently

free of poop. It seems he's finally trusted
with something he can handle, which could

lead to a promotion. As the sun sets rosily,
a south breeze billows the mainsail,

and the waves gently rock the ship,
Fool begins to feel lucky about his life

on the high seas, with its spanker booms,
bowsprits, and topgallant crosstrees.

He may sign on for another voyage
once the *Pequod*'s back in port.

Fool of the 7th Cavalry

Custer tells Fool, "We'll corral the women,
children, and old ones, who are still in camp.

Obviously, the braves won't attack, for fear
of harming their own. That's your redskin,"

he says, "too tender for the fight." Fool
wonders if someone named Crazy Horse

would be that tender. Sure enough, 3,000
Sioux, Lakota, Cheyenne, Dakota, Crow,

Kiowa, and others, including women,
fall on the 400 soldiers, shooting, stabbing,

skewering, and/or ritually mutilating all
but Fool, whose vacant stare is taken

for a shaman's gaze into the absolute.
Escorted reverently back to an encampment,

he's offered a pipe and an invitation to share
his visions with Sitting Bull, who sees

he's just a fool, who wouldn't know a vision
from a whiskey stupor. After Fool's sent away,

a charlatan convinces him to join a side show
as The Man Who Survived the Little Big Horn.

A week later, he's accidentally shot to death
by a drunk Hawaiian hired to play Crazy Horse.

Fool at High Noon

Fool finally realizes why the marshall
deputized him and then blew town.

First thing he'll have to do is buy
a gun—fast—then learn how to use it,

then try to round up some help. Trouble is
there's only half an hour before Miller

and his three goons arrive. And nobody
seems concerned about his plight. Many have

already gathered to watch the show. One guy's
vending sandwiches. It's too late to run.

If he dressed as a housewife or a granny,
somebody would probably give him away.

But surely Miller will see that Fool's not
the guy he's vowed to kill. When the moment

arrives, Miller says, "You ain't who I'm
lookin' for, but you'll do." Fool, playing

his last card, shouts, "I've got the plague,
and when your bullets hit, get ready for a dose

of plague spray, head to toe. See you
on Boot Hill, boys." When the outlaws flee,

the crowd feels relieved at first, then let down,
till they get to watch Fool cleansed in a bonfire.

Fool: Hero of the Great War

Fool takes the red-bordered draft letter
as a joke, till the marshal shows up
to escort him to boot camp, where they
shave his head and issue a uniform

three sizes too big, except for the cap,
two sizes too small. In training, he
learns that his nickname, "sad sack,"
is short for "sad sack of shit." Herded

onto a troop ship, he hears he won't
come back till it's over over there,
though he's not sure where "there" is.
There, when he's ordered "over the top,"

Fool advances dutifully with the others,
bayonets fixed, toward the enemy trench,
till an artillery blast sends him flying.
Next thing he knows he's shivering

in a shell hole, shrapnel whining
overhead. "How did I get here?"
he asks his rifle, which he was told
would be his best friend, something

he'd never had. *Pack up your troubles
in your old kit bag*, he sings, patting
his buddy on its maple butt. After he
struggles back to his outfit's trench,

he's sentenced to be shot at dawn
for desertion under fire. The colonel
tells him he can take pride in this,
since it will serve as an example

to his comrades of why they must
stay the course to victory. Fool wonders
if this could mean a medal, maybe even
a promotion, though posthumous.

Alone No More

It's Berlin right after *Kristallnackt*,
and Fool needs someone he can talk to,
someone to share his downs and
really downs. He settles for a parrot,
a green and yellow macaw he's told
speaks only Yiddish. *"Schmuck!"* it says
when he laments the water over the dam,
the money down the drain. *"Putz!"*
it barks over the upset apple carts
and spilt milk. The Groucho smile
on its beak leads Fool to look up
those words, and then some others.
"Momzer!" he fires back, *"kucker!"*

Fool feels they've found a droll way
of expressing mutual affection,
maybe love. *"Nebish,"* they squawk
at one another over a shared walnut.
It's a fair swap for the human touch,
he's thinking when the Gestapo shows up
on a tip from his snoopy neighbor.
Schmendriks! Fool shouts as a welcome
to these strangers in black leather coats,
who know Jew talk when they hear it.

Cargo Fool

—Tanna Island, South Pacific

Fool, with all his tribe, recalls the time
the G.I. Fellas, warring with the Jap Fellas,
came from the sky with Cargo, riches
they'd never seen—steel tools, tobacco,

the delicacy Spam, an elixir called
"Schlitz," and boxes that made a music
known as "Hep Cat." They mean to lure it
all back by clearing brush for a runway

lined with torches, crafting a "Longbird"
out of coconut palms, and keeping vigil
day and night. To hasten the return,
Fool dreams up three dances, the names

of which mean "Dance of the Forklift,"
"Dance of the Rubber Wheel," and
"Dance of the Typewriter." For that,
he's declared Son of John Frum, the G.I.

who brought Cargo—come "frum"
somewhere far ("E got white face,
E ride bird, E live long Amaraka")—
then packed it up and flew away.

When his tribe abandons schools,
plantation toil, and chapels to follow
the new Frum, Fool thinks he's finally
won respect and peace. He'll govern

by the Golden Rule the Christians talk
so much about. But the magistrates
arrest him, make him run a gauntlet
naked, then whisk him to another island,

where, every night, Fool scans the sky
for John Frum's second coming, when
he'll hear the Longbird's throaty call
proclaiming Cargo, Cargo, Cargo!

Fool's Errand

Dumped at midnight
from his short-sheeted cot
at Camp Tomahawk,
Tenderfoot Fool's persuaded
by his fellow Scouts
to search for the elusive snipe.
He must contemplate
the Twelve Scout Virtues,
they tell him, imitate
the Navajo, the Cree.

He takes a gunny sack,
the contradictory descriptions
and his hapless desire to please
into the rain-soaked forest.
"WooEEEP," he recites as told,
ignored by the crickets
and peepers but plunging
deeper into nature than even
the *Explorer Scout Manual* goes,
his senses strangely
magnified, his stride wily
as his brother the fox.

Tingling, he sloughs off shirt,
trousers, Jockey shorts
with the Yogi Bear elastic,
molts into a small green snake.
"Come in," sigh the trees.

"Yes," Fool's about to sibilate,
when down comes—clack!—
brother owl.

Prizewinner Fool

Fool answers the door and finds a crowd,
some men in suits in front saying they're
happy to present him with a giant check.

From the *Reader's Digest* Sweepstakes?
Fantasy Football? The Lottery? Wimbledon?
He can't remember entering any of those,

but the giant check's for serious money—
oodles of zeros—and Pricewaterhouse
certifies there can be no error. The press,

dangling boom mics, asks Fool how he
feels about his giant check. Pretty good,
he tells them. When everybody leaves, he tries

to get the giant check into his car, so he can
deposit it in his small bank account. But he
drives a Beetle, and the giant check won't

fold up. He has to rent a U-Haul van.
When he gets to his bank, the teller says,
sorry, they don't cash giant checks.

The manager confirms this, giving Fool
a suspicious look. So he wrestles the check,
which feels like it's gotten even bigger,

back into the van and drives to a larger bank,
where the teller tells him they've received
an alert from the smaller bank and have rung

for the authorities. When police arrive, they ask
Fool why he just happens to be carrying
a giant check around town, acting la-de-da,

like he thinks they're maybe blind or stupid.
Does he realize that giant checks could
be used by Moslemites to undermine

our nation's economy and that check paper
can be converted into weapons? They think
Fool could be a "Moslemite," though

his shoes look Jewboy. The bomb squad
screeches up and pitches the giant check
into the street, where they try to detonate it,

using a midget robot to probe the perimeter.
When Fool tells them it's not a bomb,
they look nonplussed, then bring out

flamethrowers, turning the giant check
into ash. "Watch your head, Ali Baba,"
says a cop, "or whatever they call you."

Fool Hits the Road

Fool hooks a ride on a tour bus occupied by
a group introducing themselves as the Seven

Deadly Sins. At first Fool thinks they must be
a punk band, though he sees no instruments.

When asked about that, the driver, Pride,
tells him, "No, we're the real deal: Envy,

Wrath, Lust, Gluttony, Avarice, Sloth, and—
best of all—yours truly." "He thinks he's

such a big shot," grumbles Envy. When
Fool asks where they're going, Lust says,

"To find some grade-A poontang, posthaste."
"What's the hurry?" says Sloth, nodding off.

"I'll hurry you, bubble ass," snarls Wrath.
"No, no, stop here!" cries Gluttony, pointing.

"It's Two-Big-Macs-for-One Day!" "Why
bother," says Sloth. Avarice, busy checking

the Dow Jones, mutters, "Damn. I knew I
should have bought Rolls Royce at $250."

"Should have bought *Whole* Foods,"
says Gluttony. Pride, shaking his head,

says, "How in God's name do I
deal with these bozos? I deserve

adoration, cringing awe." Fool says,
"God works in mysterious ways—

real mysterious, I'd say. Actually,
you sort of remind me of him."

Fool Under the Big Top

Having a knack for it already, Fool
gets hired as a sad clown, thinking

he'll touch the hearts of the crowd,
bring smiles, maybe a laugh or two.

They don't smile at the juggling,
the spritzing carnation, or the hat trick.

Nobody laughs till he gets swatted
with a slapstick, which really hurts,

or punched with a giant boxing glove,
which hurts more. When he slips

on a banana peel, his coccyx throbbing,
they roar for more, sometimes throw

peanuts and wrappers at him, demanding
bigger falls, more kicks in the behind.

Their favorite is seeing him shot
from a cannon, sailing up and into

a large pile of elephant droppings.
Fool starts to wonder if he's touched

any hearts. He might apply a smile
if he didn't think he'd lose his fans.

Fool Me Once

Fool's offered twenty acres of something called
"Tophet Glenn" by a familiar-looking man
   in line with him at the unemployment office.
"I own a lot of sunbelt real estate," says the man.
"Maybe you heard of me, Lucius Florida,
   same as the state, which was named
   after my family back in pioneer days,
   when a man's handshake was all
   you needed, and besides, money's
   not the object when it's friends,
   so sign right on this line and skip
   the fine print, the regular, too,
   just lawyer talk that'd bore
   the horns off a . . . goat, and since
   that rainy day could arrive tonight,
   why not sign up for more dough
   than the Sultan of Brunei's, *plus* total
   devotion from any babe(s) you choose
   and half off on the aluminum siding."

After Fool signs everything, he's dropped
   through a trap door into Hell. "Pathetic,"
   sighs Satan, "That's once, Fool allows."

Fool Falls Ill

Feeling woozy, Fool stops by the Acme
Urgent Care Unit in a nearby pet store,
where a trio of doctors are practicing

their Three Stooges routine for an Elks
Lodge talent show. The one playing Moe
bops him over the head with a Nerf

sledgehammer, then takes his pulse.
"Feels like a blocked cash flow," he says,
giving the Larry-one a double dog-slap.

He orders Fool to the Mercy For-Profit
Medical Center and Furniture Emporium,
where he's charged $50 an hour to stand

outside the waiting room. A chair is another
$50. Seven hours later, he's told to put on
a prison-striped hospital gown, then wheeled

on a converted Barcalounger into surgery,
done in a circus motif. A sad clown gives him
the last rites, to the tune of "I Left My Heart

in San-itation," then drops Fool's wallet
into the collection plate. While the surgeon,
Dr. Ronald McDonald, hones his scalpels,

opera-hosed nurses fiddle with a roomful
of apparati that *ca-ching* like cash registers.
Finally he declares, "Anybody named Fool

gets top billing on my A-list of specimens.
Let's *cut* a deal," he quips to canned guffaws,
"The deed to your house for my not exchanging

your brain with my Labradoodle Retriever's."
Before Fool can answer, the anesthesiologist,
former designated hitter, knocks him cold.

Fool wakes up by an alley dumpster.
behind a warehouse. "I feel better already,"
he marvels, itching for some Kibbles 'n Bits.

Tattered Fool

An Horatio Alger Narrative

Fool has to give up school to care for
his widowed mother in their shanty
on the edge of town. He delivers milk,
newspapers, and mail, persevering

at the three jobs during rain, snow,
and scorching heat, wearing only his
tattered work clothes, too-small
gauzy-soled shoes, and plucky smile.

During a record-setting blizzard,
an oil tycoon happens to spot
Fool's hand protruding from a drift,
waving the evening edition.

"Extra," shouts the muffled voice.
That boy's got spunk, thinks the tycoon,
the kind he's looking for in his search
for a son-in-law worthy of taking over

the business. "You're hired," he shouts
at the drift. Fool's then introduced
to the tycoon's daughter, a stunning beauty
who likes the cut of Fool's jib. Marriage

follows and a fast track to vice president.
But the tycoon acts as if he's God,
demanding obedience and adulation
from everyone. And he expects Fool

to spy on the others. Fool finds this,
plus the required three-piece herringbone
and power tie, a tight fit. And he's baffled
about which fork to use on what serving

at the country club dinners. Rebellion's
reached the boiling point company-wide
when one of the other V.P.s, plotting
a hostile takeover, invites Fool to join.

"We'll turn this hellhole into a heaven,"
he whispers, "though we might have to skirt
some regulations," which sounds good to Fool,
despite an unsettling sense of déjà vu.

Delivering books, papers, and magazines
from his cart to the other inmates, Fool
enjoys the exercise and clarity of purpose,
whistling as he makes his plucky rounds.

The Frog Fool

Fool's motoring down Santa Monica Boulevard
when he notices large pop-eyes in a green forehead
staring back in the rear view mirror. "RIBBIT!"

he roars, to his surprise, calling for help. As his car
slows and traffic backs up, he tries charade signals:
Sounds like . . . ! SOUNDS LIKE . . . ! he flippers

wildly to his fellow commuters, who don't
stop honking or flashing birds and fists.
It doesn't help that they're seeing a giant frog.

Will the office notice? Can he find loafers that fit?
Will his bowling league still sanction him?
Fool wonders, watching his elastic tongue

snick a fly off the dashboard. He feels
a deep desire to be French kissed
by a nubile beauty of royal birth.

But the only girl nearby is screaming for him
to go fuck himself. Fool abandons his car,
hops down an alley, and hides in a dumpster,

which Sanitation later empties into
one of its trucks. As he wonders how he'll
get cleaned up for romance, the truck

dumps him in a landfill, on a mound
of soiled Pampers. There's no sign of his lady.
My torrid blood's gone cold, he laments

in Frog, though his now familiar tongue
feasts on the multitude of ambient flies, which,
his new brain notes, are much bigger and juicier

than the one on the dashboard. When the bulldozer
pancakes him in mid-munch, he's dreaming
jeweled tiara, olive skin, webbed toes.

Playing the Fool

Fool combines a Gibson and a trombone, which,
after considering "Gibsbone" and "Trombson,"
and "Bonegib," he decides to name it after himself.

The Fool sounds as if a combination boat horn
and air-raid klaxon were lodged in the inner ear,
repelling everyone at his first and only concert.

But war game stategists invite him to do
a test "firing" against fifty unsuspecting
subjects, who all run screaming in surrender.

He's drafted into Delta Force, but when he
aims "Eye of the Tiger" at an ISIS base,
even his comrades flee from the hellish yawp.

Crestfallen, he segues into "Alone Again,"
causing seven nearby villages, even their deaf
and infeebled, to evacuate helter-skelter.

Fool wonders if something less apocalyptic
could attract some fans. A piccolo-ukelele
might do: Picolele, Ukelolo, Oloukilo?

The New Boss

Fool buys a learn-to-play-guitar book
at a local Walgreens, and after mastering
lessons one and two, sees a late-night TV ad
for the Ajax Music Agency. At the audition,

he's told that, with their "Apex Plan,"
a mega-career in rock 'n' roll will be
a gimme once he pays the two grand
to get his act into the major venues.

At his first gig, Peoria's Chugalug Lounge,
he gets a jolting shock from his Gibson knockoff,
which sends his right hand into a frenetic
palsy, producing a marvel of turbo meedlies.

Word spreads till Fool, now known as
"The Boss Man of Meedly," and his group,
Short Circuit, are wowing thousands
in major coliseums. After every concert,

they have to jostle their way through
showers of bras and panties to get to
a stretch limo waiting to whisk them
to a trendy hotel and yet another night

of sex, booze, and cocaine. This goes on
till Fool smashes his trusty guitar
on a tray of Dom Perignon and has to
get a new one. At the following concert

his blundering, unpalsied solos draw
boos, catcalls, and after a few more gigs,
obscurity. Fool later dies trying to construct
a guitar he planned to call The Electicutioner.

Laureate Fool

After trying to write a couple of poems,
Fool decides to submit them to a trendy

literary magazine, failing to notice he's
mixed them up with his grocery list:

Orange Nehi, Cap'n Crunch, Velveeta,
SpaghettiOs, Hamburger Helper,

Moon Pies. Almost at once, he gets
an acceptance letter praising the depth

of his "edgy ellipticity" and saying he's
been awarded the Breakthrough Prize.

The next issue contains an analysis
of the poem, lauding its plunge beneath

the rational world and into "the vortex
of chaotic indeterminacy, the tintinnabular

cacophony of sound, and the absolute
abdication of sense, all of that done

with what at first seems an everyday
catalog but which blooms into a vehicle

for a profound ontology." The writer ends
calling for a full collection. Fool,

always eager to please, assembles
a book-length grocery list, which requires

considerable repetition. Raves echo
throughout the world of avant-garde

poetics, especially for the repetition,
which is said to launch a new poetic style,

or, to the initiated, Anti-style. Heartened,
Fool composes an epic consisting

of the letter F repeated for 900 lines.
Though he's then run over by a fire truck,

he dies assured his lines will live on
in the hearts of poetry's dozen-or-so readers.

Fool Visits the All-New Hell

Though things look and smell pretty much
the same, Satan tells Fool he's finally made
Hell a heaven, declared it a theme park
called Six Flags over Pandemonium.

Now it's the River Kicks instead of Styx,
and the Lake of Fire's become Cosy Springs.
He says, "Once you bend through Limbo,
(How low can you go?), the real fun begins."

When Fool asks about the cries of the damned,
he's told they're "joy squeals." "We've added
nine new amusement levels," says Satan. "There's
a boiling-pitch slide on Six and a Harpy-Go-Round

on Eight. Our ad boys, Moloch, Belial, Mammon,
and Beelzebub, have hatched a new campaign:
Surprise The Wife with a New Burning Coffin.
We've hit pay dirt. People are lining up at the gates

for Hat Day, and our time shares are off the charts."
Fool puts a down payment on one with a deluxe
molten-brimstone tub and view of the River Lethe,
floral-scented and renamed The Forget-me-not.

Fool Visits the All-New Heaven

When Fool asks why, God declares
the perpetual worship thing was getting
pretty old for everybody. Perfection, too,
since nothing could ever change without
creating imperfection. Fool notices

a proclamation slapped on the Pearly Gates
announcing "Open Admissions," St. Peter
absent. Replacing The Heavenly Chorus
is Battle of the Bands, today featuring
Lawrence Welk and the Hotsy Totsy Boys

vs. Jan "Idol of the Airwaves" Garber
and his Musical Clowns. Señor Wences
and Benny Hill provide the knee-slappers.
For those whose spirits need uplifting,
there's Al Jolson's blackface version

of "Mammy." "I get teary every time I hear
him belt the finish," says God. "And when
that band America dies off, we'll have them
doing marathons of 'Horse with No Name.'
It says a lot between the lines," He says.

Though resident souls can now eat
white bread and grape juice for all,
God's heard a lot of new ones opt for Hell.
"I don't get it," He says. "Me neither,"
says Fool. "Maybe do Bingo Night."

Fool Discovers the Meaning of Life

Fool, demoted to heavenly custodian
after failing to keep the system on line

during God's weekly trip to ensure
the gates of Hell stay bolted tight,

has trouble staying busy in a realm
too perfect to have trash or sewage.

All he can do is putter around
God's Study, moving the Holy Chair

from behind His Cathedral-sized Desk,
then moving It back. He'd dust, if there

were any in Heaven. But he can't resist
taking a peek into God's Filing Cabinet,

where everything's kept in Perfect Order.
He thumbs through "Vengeance," thickest

of the lot, cataloging fires, quakes,
eruptions, and floods, plus some fancy

stuff like neurofibromatosis, yaws,
and Hurler syndrome. Next comes

"Petty Amusements," listing fleas,
termites, leeches, and Fox News. Then,

"Speeches," orated to Moses, Abraham,
Job, and the like. And after that, sealed

with Divine Wax: "The Meaning of Life."
Breathless, Fool breaks the seal, whereupon

a cherub choir flutters up and a colossal
safe marked "600 Tons" crepes him.

Fool Gives a Commencement Address

He was just supposed to test the mic,
but after a few taps and puffs, he can't
resist a chance to offer those fresh faces
his special brand of street savvy. First,
he warns them not to trust those emails

from a supposed Nigerian ex-bigwig
offering you a million dollars to help him
transfer his billions to America—if you'll
wire him $1,500 for "incidentals." Fool
did that last year, and may report it

as a scam, though it might only seem
to be, and then he's flushed a million
down the crapper. Life, he notes, is
complicated. Sometimes, you meet
yourself coming and going, a saying

that's also not always true. So there
you are. When he was a boy, they had
Boy Scouts, which wasn't any picnic,
but Scoutmasters then wouldn't try
to bugger you, and you could learn a lot

of knots. The assholes, he tells them, seem
to always get rich and win elections. But
carry on. That million might arrive
tomorrow, he shouts over his shoulder
as Security applies the bum's rush.

World's Best-Kept Secret

It's that Fool's been in charge ever since
God opted to turn things over to him
after the Fall, taking early retirement
to an unlisted galaxy, where he plays golf

and watches *Lamp Unto My Feet* reruns.
Fires, floods, earthquakes, cancer, wars,
etc.? The Divine Mechanism, which Deists
likened to a jazzy Swiss watch, is just

too intricate for Fool, who still has
trouble tying his shoelaces and finding
the little doohickie that switches the station
from AM to FM. And, of course, he's not

always on duty. In fact, he's granted,
sometimes for decades, breaks on earth,
during which more trains run on time
and explosions, mass shootings, and pileups

of twenty or more cars don't happen
so often. The air, too, clears somewhat.
But he always ends up getting lynched
or worse, and then it's back to business

in the Hereafter. The Lisbon Earthquake,
the one that killed maybe 100,000? Fool
was too busy then trying to start those
April showers that bring May flowers,

which later caused the Johnstown Flood.
Vesuvius? Fool believed RED indicated
the pressure gages were working just fine.
World War II? Fool thought "blitzkrieg"

was German for "hot sex" and Hirohito
was an extra-large mojito. And so we
suffer Fool, our brother who art in heaven,
though not all the time, thank God.

Biographical Note

Call Me Fool is William Trowbridge's ninth poetry collection. His poems have appeared in more than forty-five anthologies and textbooks, as well as on *The Writer's Almanac* and *American Life in Poetry*, and in such periodicals as *Poetry*, *The Gettysburg Review*, *The Georgia Review*, *The Southern Review*, *Plume*, *Rattle*, *The Iowa Review*, *Prairie Schooner*, *Epoch*, and *New Letters*. He lives in the Kansas City area and teaches in the University of Nebraska Low-residency MFA in Writing Program. He was Poet Laureate of Missouri from 2012 to 2016.

CPSIA information can be obtained
at www.ICGtesting.com
Printed in the USA
JSHW022231250722
28441JS00003B/8